the Feast of Enemies

COMMUNION MEDITATIONS
KENNETH L. GIBBLE

Lima, Ohio
C.S.S. Publishing Company

Unless otherwise noted, the Scripture texts are taken from the *Revised Standard Version* of the Bible.

0635/ISBN 0-89536-671-1

11/86 2.05T
PRINTED IN U.S.A.

CONTENTS

Hunger of the Heart

John 6:27-35

"Man does not live by bread alone." That's certainly one of the most familiar of all quotations. Like so many well-known sayings, it comes from the Bible and, in particular, from the confrontation Jesus had with Satan in the wilderness.

I'm sure you remember the story. How Jesus, after he had been baptized in the Jordan River by his cousin John, was led by the Spirit into a lonely place. There he prepared himself for his ministry with prayers and fasting. The tempter came to him then.

> "If you are the Son of God," he said, "command this stone to be made bread." Jesus answered, "It is written, 'Man shall not live by bread alone ...'" (Luke 4:1-4)

Jesus' answer was a quotation from the book of Deuteronomy, where Moses tells the people that God's feeding them manna in the wilderness was to prove to them that he, the Lord God, was their provider. Moses says to the people:

> "Man does not live by bread alone, but ... by everything that proceeds out of the mouth of the Lord." (Deuteronomy 8:3)

I believe we twentieth century Americans have

had the opportunity to see the truth of this biblical affirmation in a way unparalleled by any other people in human history. We have been able to see first-hand that, indeed, "man does *not* live by bread alone."

We are well-fed people. Too well-fed, in many cases. Ever since the human race got started, people have dreamed of a life free from the fear of starvation. For the great majority of Americans, that dream is a reality. And since the struggle for food to eat is the most basic of all, one would think that a people whose physical needs have been met would live happy, contented, fulfilled lives.

But it hasn't worked that way, has it? You and I read in our newspapers and magazines about glamorous people who have all that life can offer in terms of material abundance; yet all too often they are still searching for something more. They desperately embrace the latest cure-all offered by the gurus and pop psychologists that proliferate the scene. But nothing ever seems to give the lasting sense of inner peace they long for.

We ourselves know that bread alone isn't enough to live on. We set goals for ourselves — getting the car paid off, buying a house, building up that savings account. But when we achieve them, we are no closer than before to a sense of real fulfillment.

"Man does not live by bread alone." It's true. We see it and experience it and know it to be true.

And it is from this truth that the bread of that blessed meal we call Holy Communion derives its meaning. The bread of which we partake as we come to the Lord's Table is rich in symbolic meanings. It betokens many things — the productivity of the earth which God has given for our welfare, the bread which Jesus shared with his disciples in the upper room in Jerusalem, his own body broken for our salvation, the body of believers which is the church universal. All these images and meanings cluster around the bread we shall eat.

But there is yet another meaning. We find it in a phrase from the Gospel of John. The word had gotten out that Jesus had fed a multitude with five loaves and two fish. On the next day, another crowd flocks to him. Looking at the people, Jesus knows what has attracted them. And he knows too that bread made from flour will not satisfy their deepest hunger, the hunger of the heart.

And so he tells them that what they really need is life-giving bread from God himself. Then he makes the claim which Christian believers have cherished from that time to this. Jesus says:

"I am the bread of life; he who comes to me shall not hunger."

My friends, we are no different from those people who came to Jesus. They thought they knew what they wanted. But he knew them better than they knew themselves.

God knows us that way too — outside and in, backwards and forwards. He knows the hunger of our hearts, and in his son Jesus, he supplies our need. Our need for acceptance and forgiveness and love and hope.

In Christ he bids us come and eat. We eat trusting him, believing in his promises, celebrating the joy that comes in being known and loved by him.

It is with deep gladness that we hear the invitation from our Lord: "Come and eat; for this is the bread of life."

4

By Invitation Only

A MEDITATION FOR WORLD WIDE COMMUNION

Isaiah 56:6-8 and Luke 14:16-24

George Babbitt, the all-too-much-like-us character created by the pen of Sinclair Lewis, had hit upon a brilliant plan. He presented it proudly to his wife at the supper table.

"Now you know how important it is for my business and for our — well — social standing that we get invited to dinner by the Caulwells. Until we can get into their circle of acquaintances, we're just nobodies. I mean, that's where the influence and prestige is *at*. So I've come up with this idea, see. I told you, Henry and I — Henry Caulwell, that is — were in college together. So when I go to the alumni reception next week, I'll approach Henry on the basis of being old classmates you know — that kind of thing — and I'll invite him and his missus over for dinner. What do you say to that?"

Mrs. Babbitt, dear trusting soul, was once again nearly overwhelmed with admiration for her husband's knowledge of the affairs of the world. And so she drew up her invitation list which had the Caulwell's name prominently at the top. In a weak moment, the Caulwells accepted the invitation. When the night of the party arrived, George Babbitt was so nervous, he just couldn't sit still. He was constantly moving about, doing his utmost to be the affable host.

But somehow, the party didn't come off. The Caulwells left early — a bad sign. And the Babbitts waited in vain for the return invitation.

One evening several months later Babbitt said to his wife over dessert, "You know, I'm kinda glad we never got invited by the Caulwells. That crowd they're in is just a bunch of stuffed shirts anyhow."

George Babbitt's experience probably reminds you of some similar event in your own life. Very few of us escape the disappointment of not being invited to something we wished desperately to attend. What can match the tearful misery of a little girl who learns she will not be a guest at the big birthday party of a classmate? It's a terrible feeling to know you are excluded, isn't it?

Maybe that's why the Christian message has been such Good News to all kinds of people down through the centuries. There is in the invitation of the church — when it is faithful to its Lord — an absence of any qualifiers. You don't have to speak a certain language or have an income above a certain level or have the right family background or have at least a high school education or wear a certain style of clothes. No, it's a "whoever will, may come" proposition.

The note is sounded in the prophet Isaiah. For a long time, the Hebrews had made their religion a restrictive one: no foreigners, no outsiders. But the age is dawning, says the prophet for the Lord God, when foreigners shall come to the holy mountain and be joyful in the house of prayer. For thus says the Lord God, "My house shall be called a house of prayer for all people."

Today is the occasion when the Christian church celebrates World Wide Communion. It is a day when we bring to mind the literally millions of Christians who join us at the Lord's Table to eat the bread and drink the wine which makes us one in Christ. Think for a moment of the diversity of people who eat and drink with us today: people of every nation and race. How the prophecy of Isaiah has been fulfilled!

So often in our Christian experience we focus attention on ourselves. We think and plan in terms of our congregation, our house of worship, our community. Too much of that is very dangerous. We start having such a wonderful time with our own little group that we miss the opportunity and blessing that lie outside ourselves. We forget that we are invited to kneel at the Lord's Table that we may be strengthened to rise again and go out to spread the love of Christ to all we meet.

The invitation we receive is both a gift and a challenge. In the story Jesus told about a man who planned a big banquet, there were those who thought of the invitation only in terms of the obligation it placed on them. They gave all kinds of reasons for excusing themselves. But those who accepted the invitation to the banquet were those who really appreciated it and gained much from it; the poor and maimed and blind.

In a sense, all of us who respond to the invitation to the Lord's Table are also poor and maimed and blind. Not one of us is really good enough to partake of the communion of Christ's body and blood. And so when we realize that presence at the Lord's Table is by invitation only, we can be deeply thankful that it's Christ himself who gives the invitation. He knows the sin that mars our lives. He knows what makes us hurt inside, what keeps us from being truly free people, what stands in the way of our spiritual well-being. But he doesn't ask that we be perfect before he gives his invitation. He asks only that we come in humility, having confessed our sin, and that we be willing to allow God to renew our hearts.

Here's to the Kingdom!

Luke 22:7-20

What does the bread and the wine of Holy Communion mean to you?

This is an important question for any Christian, and because it is, I am going to ask you to think about it for a short period. Let's spend some time in silent reflection as we each try to answer this question for ourselves:

"What does the bread and wine of Holy Communion mean to me?"

Most of us have been taking Communion for years, but often we do it automatically without pausing to ask ourselves what it is we are doing. No doubt the thoughts of each of you were unique, but we can be fairly certain that several common themes came to mind.

For many of us, the symbols of the bread and wine are representative of the broken body and shed blood of our Lord on Calvary. For others of us, the Communion has special meaning as a meal shared with friends and loved ones of this faith community. For still others, emphasis falls on the gift of inward strength which God imparts through these symbols, strength to face the difficulties that confront us from day to day.

All these and many other meanings Christians have found in the bread and the cup. It is a rich and full sacrament, an outward, visible act which contains an inward, invisible grace.

As we hear the Scripture about the last meal Jesus shared with his companions just prior to his arrest and trial, we sense that those at the table that night knew that this was indeed a special meal. And we wonder: Did the disciples understand what Jesus was doing as he broke the bread and poured the wine?

How *could* they have understood? Only later, when he had suffered and died and then been raised, could they grasp fully what he had told them. I find it interesting that the earliest manuscripts of the Gospels show variations in what was said at the Last Supper. Some of them record the words of Jesus as we find them in Luke's Gospel. Others add that Jesus, after he had given his friends the bread and the cup, said to them: "Do this in remembrance of me."

So we cannot come to the Lord's Table without remembering, without looking back in time.

And yet, the thrust of Luke's account of the Last Supper is not a backward look, but a *forward* one. Jesus says of the bread:

"*I shall not eat it (again) until it is fulfilled in the kingdom of God.*"

And of the wine he says:

"*. . . from now on I shall not drink of the fruit of the vine until the kingdom of God comes.*"

We often miss this forward thrust of the Communion. And that's unfortunate. For Jesus, the Last Supper was not a solemn farewell nearly so much as a toast to the future. It's almost as though he raised the cup and said to his friends: "Here's to the kingdom!"

Jesus believed that the suffering and death which awaited him would, by God's power, be turned into a victory over evil. That, at least in part, was his understanding of God's kingdom. And so he said to his followers:

> "As my Father appointed a kingdom for me, so do I appoint for you that you may eat and drink at my table in the kingdom . . . " (Luke 22:29-30)

Earlier he had said:

> "Men will come from east and west, and from north and south, and sit at table in the kingdom of God." (Luke 13:29)

Exactly what Jesus imagined this banquet to be, we cannot know. We have only brief glimpses of it in the Gospels.

Neither can we know what God's kingdom will be when his divine purpose is fulfilled. But as Christians, we have faith that time and human existence and our own lives are not a meaningless parade of years and events. We believe that in his own good time, God will bring to completion that work begun in Jesus who was Christ.

And so for us, the bread and the cup are a remembrance of Jesus and his sacrifice. But not only a remembrance.

They also become an appetizer, a foretaste of that which awaits us when the living Lord will eat and drink with us. It is this faith that enables us to come to the Table on this day with hope and joy. It is this same faith we celebrate when we sing the words to the old hymn: "Blessed assurance, Jesus is mine! O what a foretaste of glory divine!"

My brothers and sisters in Christ: "Here's to the Kingdom!"

Bread for the World

Matthew 14:13-21

What really happened on that lakeside so many years ago? How was it that more than 5,000 people were fed by our Lord?

Some Christians look for a literal meaning. They believe that by his divine power, Jesus produced from the few loaves and fish enough for all to eat with food left over.

Others see the story as evidence of a symbolic meal. They see the similarity between this story and the account of how Jesus broke bread with his disciples at the Last Supper. Each of the 5,000 took only a small morsel, much as we do at Communion, and that these morsels, blessed by our Lord, conveyed such power and grace that all who partook were satisfied in their innermost beings.

Still other Christians interpret the story to mean that Jesus was able to inspire a spirit of sharing among those present. Many in the crowd had brought a meal for themselves but had no intentions of sharing with their neighbors. But when Jesus took the lunch that a young boy had offered, blessed it and began to break the loaves, those who had food were moved to do the same so that all had enough and to spare.

How the miracle was accomplished we do not know, for the Gospel does not tell us. But miracle there was, whether we think of it as a physical manifestation of divine power, as a spiritual miracle satisfying the deepest longings of Jesus' hearers, or as a miracle changing the selfishness of people into a sharing fellowship of love.

Commenting on this story, Dr. William Felmeth of Princeton Seminary notes that it reveals truths about God's will for humankind that are important for us today. First is the obvious truth that God cares what happens to people's bodies. God isn't just interested in our souls, but in our whole selves. The Creator made us of flesh and blood; it is his will that the physical needs of all his children be cared for. Those of us whose needs are met dare not ignore human suffering — illness, ignorance, hunger. We cannot excuse ourselves by saying they are only natural in a world such as ours. In the words of the apostle James: "If a brother or sister is ill-clad and in lack of daily food, and one of you says to them, 'Go in peace, be warmed and filled,' without giving them the things needed for the body, what good is it?"

Like the disciples, we may be troubled by the world's hungry and needy. Like them, we think in our hearts, "Send them away." But then Christ says to us as he did to the twelve, "You feed them." We who are his followers must have the same concern for the suffering, the hungry, as did he who is our Lord.

A second truth we can discover is that God stands ready to use whatever we have to offer to accomplish his purposes. All the disciples could bring was the lunch of a little boy, who had himself given what little he had. Yet that little, in the Master's hands, became the much that satisfied many. So too can our gifts, as inadequate as we may feel they are, be used by God. "Bring them here to me," he says, and he will enlarge whatever we bring — our talents, our work, our resources, our lives — and make of them more than we ever believed possible.

A third truth we have from the Gospel story is one

we understand most clearly at special moments —
such as the Holy Communion — that through Jesus
Christ, God satisfies the hunger within us. He tells us
to pray for daily bread, physical bread, yes; but he
also asks, "Is life not more than food?" We spend so
much of our time and money on the physical, yet we
are dissatisfied. Something is missing, lacking. We tell
ourselves that we are "fed up" with our lives, and yet
we are starving, starving because our souls have not
been fed. We need to hear the gracious words of our
Lord: "I am the bread of life. They who come to me
shall never hunger and they who believe in me shall
never thirst."

As we approach the Lord's Table this day, we must
remember that we come in our need. We need
sustenance from God. We should remember, too, our
Christian sisters and brothers in every land who join us
in partaking of the bread and the cup. Finally, let us
remember still others who do not come but await even
the crumbs from the table — a vast multitude, who
are hungry physically and, like us, hungry spiritually.

So we share the bread of life at this table with our
Lord, and with each other, and with the whole world.

Of Flags and Nations . . . and a Table

Isaiah 66:18-21

"I pledge allegiance to the flag of the United States of America . . ."

Most of us learned to say those words as children without thinking. As adults, on the rare occasions we recite the Pledge of Allegiance, we still do so without paying much attention to what it is we are saying.

As I understand it, the whole idea of pledging allegiance has its roots in the ancient tradition of a defeated warrior swearing an oath of loyalty to his victorious enemy. The sacred oath was a means of insuring that the defeated person or tribe would not strike a blow of retaliation as soon as the conquering army turned its attention to other foes.

Now, as a youngster, the implications of pledging allegiance never occurred to me. That is, until I learned that one of my friends, a boy about my age, who came from a Mennonite family, suffered ridicule from the other kids because he was forbidden to say the Pledge of Allegiance. "Why don't his parents want him to pledge allegiance?" I asked my dad. "Well," he explained, "they believe it's wrong to give allegiance to anyone except the Lord." I couldn't comprehend that — at least not until many years later.

I still say the Pledge of Allegiance. But on those public occasions when I do so, I never fail to think of my boyhood friend, and I always have the uncomfortable feeling that his refusal was nearer the mark than my acquiescence. I love my country, but that's not the issue. The issue for me is that any institution which insists on my allegiance must recognize that my primary allegiance is to the God I worship and the Christ I obey.

Every time I say the Pledge of Allegiance, there is one phrase in particular that sticks in my throat. "One nation, under God." That's the one — *under God.* It was added to the Pledge when I was still a student in public school. We stumbled over it then because it was new and sounded strange. I stumble over it now because it disturbs me profoundly. It carries the sanctimonious odor of arrogance and idolatry.

Let me explain. I object to the phrase because it is the rankest of hypocrisies to suppose that we are indeed united in our worship of Almighty God. Polls tell us that a majority of Americans believe in God. The same polls reveal that such belief has nearly nothing to do with worship habits or behavior patterns. We are not a "Christian nation," and we never have been, despite all the rhetoric to the contrary.

But my foremost objection comes with the subtle assertion implicit in the phrase, "one nation, under God." It is the notion that God is on *our side.* God looks upon us with special favor in marked contrast to the Russians or the Iranians or whoever the bad guys of the moment happen to be. It is the self-same error the people of ancient Israel made. God is on our side, they assumed, and no wonder. For, after all, they said, we are just a bit more religious and generous and good than anybody else.

But the prophets uttered a loud and forceful "NO" to that notion. They proclaimed a universal God to a people of a particularist mentality. Not one nation under God, but *all* nations under God. The prophet called Third Isaiah speaks for the Lord: "I am coming to gather all nations and tongues . . . " (Isaiah 66:18)

Jesus carried the prophet's message a step further. A good religious person asked him, "Lord, will those who are saved be few?" Jesus responded with an answer that made his listeners wince. It isn't the ones who think they've got it made who get into the Kingdom. At the Kingdom feast, the tables are turned. Publicans and prostitutes are invited in ahead of the high-brow religious leaders (Matthew 21:31).

Jesus also said to his listeners: You think because you are children of Abraham that you've got a corner on God's favor. But you are wrong. People will come from east and west and north and south from all nations and races and cultures and sit at table in the Kingdom of God (Luke 13:29).

If we can bear it, we can hear Jesus telling us that being successful people, being Americans, being proper Christians, counts for exactly nothing in God's regard. At the Lord's table, the human credentials of status, wealth, and all the rest, are null and void. If anything, those credentials can keep us off the guest list. Not because God hates them or us, but because in our own eyes they have become too important. We think they somehow make us "better than."

No. Not one nation under God, *our* nation . . . but all nations. Not one kind of people at the Lord's table, *our* kind of people . . . but *all* people. The invitations to the banquet are based on God's grace, not our own merit. In great humility and gratitude, then, we come to the Lord's Table, rejoicing that we are Christ's welcome guests, that he loves even the likes of us. Wonder of wonders. Even the likes of us!

We in Christ; Christ in Us

John 6:51-63

In our day of church buildings dotting the American landscape, of Christianity acknowledged (at least in theory) as *the* religion of most Americans, it is easy to forget that the Christian church, for the first century or so of its fragile life, was an underground movement. That is, Christians often could not worship in public for fear of persecution. The secrecy demanded of each Christian believer soon led to fear and suspicion on the part of outsiders. What were those Christians *doing* when they met for their sacred rituals? What dark, unnameable practices did they engage in?

Frequently, just enough of their worship rituals became known to inflame the imaginations of their critics. One outspoken critic listed some of the abominable practices carried on by the adherents of this strange new religion. He observed that the Christians emphasized the word LOVE. He concluded, therefore, that they engaged in sexual debaucheries — and that, no doubt, is a revealing commentary on his concept of love. He was especially appalled because Christians called each other "brother" and "sister"; he believed they used those terms so as to compound their wickedness by adding incest to their crimes. Then he described in gruesome detail a supposed Christian practice which he no doubt took delight in fabricating. He tells how they practiced cannibalism at their banquets, eating human flesh and drinking human blood. And he writes of this horror: "The sacred rites are more foul than any sacrilege." (Quoted in *A History of Christianity*, Ray C. Petry, ed., Prentice-Hall, 1962, p. 41.)

We all know what exaggeration and misunderstanding can lead to. Obviously, someone had heard that the Christians partook of the body and blood of the Lord Jesus as they celebrated the Eucharist, and so it isn't at all surprising that an outsider should conclude they practiced cannibalism. It is especially not surprising when we read in the Gospel of John that some of Jesus' followers misinterpreted his words on this subject.

Jesus, in words similar to what the other Gospels record as his statement at the Last Supper, says:

> "My flesh is real food and my blood is real drink. He who eats my flesh and drinks my blood lives in me and I in him."

After hearing this, many of his followers said, "This is intolerable language. How could anyone accept it?"

They too did not understand what Jesus meant. The horrible thought of cannibalism sprang to their minds. And so Jesus said to them:

> "It is the spirit that gives life, the flesh has nothing to offer. The words I have spoken to you are spirit, and they are life." (John 6:55 ff. Jerusalem Bible)

This Scripture from John is important to us as we anticipate kneeling at the Lord's Table and partaking of the bread and cup. We discover, from John's Gospel, that the bread is not literally the body of Christ, just as the juice of the grape is not literally his blood. They remain common elements — by partaking of them our sins will not be magically erased and our lives be made pure and beautiful.

No, the importance of the Holy Communion lies in what it *signifies*. What it signifies for us is, first of all, our recognition of who Jesus was — the one sent from God to reveal to us God's power and love. When we come to the table, we do so affirming that in some unique, mysterious way, God was in Christ, drawing us to himself. We recall how Christ gave himself for us, fully and lovingly. We accept this gift humbly, knowing full well that we do not deserve such love, not with all the sin that clings to us. So we come to the table, grateful beyond words for God's mercy.

But the bread and the cup signify something else for us too. They betoken our desire that the spirit of Christ enter our lives, that we partake of his life, that Christ may live in us and we may live in him. So it is that our partaking of the elements is a declaration of intention — our intention to be Christlike in our words and thoughts and actions.

Jesus says:

"He who eats my flesh and drinks my blood lives in me and I in him."

Is that what you desire — that you may live in Christ and he in you? If you do, that means you will receive his strength, his power. If you do, that means you must put away those things in you which are not Christlike: pettiness, unkind words, prejudice, irresponsible behavior.

If you want to live in Christ and he in you, then come to the table and partake of his body and blood — for he bids you come.

A Table Set for the World

A MEDITATION FOR WORLD WIDE COMMUNION

Isaiah 25:6-8

The Christmas table at my Grandpa Ober's house was a sight to behold. For one thing, the amount of food on it was enough to buckle the legs of your run of the mill table. On it were assorted vegetables, noodles, breads, and desserts — and of course the turkey.

But the most striking feature of the table was its length. Under several white tablecloths, it stretched the whole length of the dining room, through the French doors and into the parlor, which on all other occasions was an unused room. And when all the children, grandchildren, and in-laws had assembled, we numbered upwards of forty or so.

Grandpa's house rested on the top of a rise and so had to bear the brunt of the wintry wind which invariably howled at the windows on Christmas Day. Inside all was warmth, friendly chatter, and us children's excitement as we explained what we had gotten for Christmas presents. But it was the meal itself that I remember best.

After all the preparations were ended, every squirming youngster had been shushed, and every baby fastened to his or her high chair, Grandpa Ober, seated at the head of the table, would lower his chin into his white beard and thank God for food and health and the blessing of the large family gathered at the table. There was a feeling of solidarity, of unity about it. We had individual identities that were recognized and respected, but we were one family — we belonged here. Above all, we were loved, knew we were loved, and we loved gladly in return.

Having shared Christmas dinner around Grandpa and Grandma's table, we were linked to one another in some indescribable way for the rest of our lives. We had our squabbles, of course. There were some jealousies and rivalries. Cousin Paul and I once nearly came to blows when a friendly wrestling match threatened to turn into a free-for-all. Grandpa sometimes played favorites. But when we were gathered around the table, we all knew that this is how it was meant to be, that we were, in fact, a part of each other.

There is another table I want to talk about this morning. It too is a very long table. It has been set and extends from here all the way around the world. On this day, World Communion Sunday, when everyone has assembled around it, we will number in the millions. The food at this table is simple fare — just bread and wine — and there are some of us who will have little else to eat today except this bread and wine. But all who come to the table know that it's not the actual food that matters, but the meaning attached to it.

The people around this table come in various sizes and colors. Some are young, some old. Most of us are in good health, but a few are so near to death that the bread must be placed in their mouths, the wine held to their lips. The people around this table have different opinions on many subjects. Some are stout defenders of the free enterprise system; some are avowed Marxists. Some believe that the proper way to come to the table is in repentant sorrow; others come with glad smiles for the joy they feel.

But despite our differences, we have one thing in common. We know that the meal is an act of God's grace on our behalf. In Christ, we become one family. We know that above all else, this is a meal of love: first, of Christ's love for us, and second, of the love we share with each other. And as we surround the table, we know that this is how it was meant to be.

The Lord's table means even more than this, however. In a sense, it is also a prelude of things to come, a vision first seen by the prophet Isaiah when he foretold a banquet of rich fare for all people, prepared by God himself. In what way and time that table will be set, God alone knows. But we pray earnestly for its coming. Some call it the Kingdom of God. Christ himself will eat and drink with us as he promised his disciples in an upstairs room years ago in Jerusalem.

And we *do* long for that table to be set for the whole world. We've had our fill of terrorism and hatred and wars and dread of nuclear annihilation. We come to the Lord's table today confessing the part we play in the brokenness of our world. But we come also with faith and hope — faith that the oneness we share with fellow-Christians is God's will for his people, and hope that the table will soon be surrounded by all our sisters and brothers.

But What Does It Mean?

Mark 14:17-25

Symbols and rituals are important. No less than our ancestors in past time, we need them today. We need them to maintain our continuity with the past. We need them to give us a sense of the orderliness of our existence. We need them to express the human joys and longings that words are inadequate to express.

But there is a problem with symbols and rituals. They wear out. It doesn't take long — often less than a generation — for the original meaning behind the ritual to be lost. And so if someone asks, "What does this visual symbol or that gesture *mean?*" chances are, no one will really know.

Let me give you a case in point. A few months ago, someone on our Worship Committee asked: "What is the meaning of the way the acolyte nods the taper in front of the cross when lighting the candles?" And none of us knew the answer. Oh, we had lots of ideas about what it *might* mean, but they were educated guesses at best. What we could all agree on was: "Well, that's the way it's always been done."

Now when it comes to the matter of religious symbols, it seems to me that such an answer isn't really good enough. In each generation, we need to reexamine our symbols, our rituals. As we teach them to our children and to those who join our fellowship, we must ask, again and again: Where did they come from? What *did* they mean? What do they mean now? Are they still useful and valid?

One of the most important rituals in the Christian church is called Holy Communion. There are other names for it too, but most of us, when we hear the words "Holy Communion," bring to mind certain things — things like the bread and the cup, the story of Jesus and the disciples in the upper room, the broken body and shed blood of our Lord.

Partly because I have always been interested in such things, and partly because I wonder what significance this ritual has for members of this congregation, I have begun to explore some of its meanings. The place to begin, of course, is with the Scriptures. From there we look into our church tradition, until finally we come to our own participation in and practice of the Communion. I have really only begun my study, but I've already made some discoveries.

One discovery is that every ritual is based on a key event in history. For a religious ritual, like Communion, we naturally look for an event recorded in the Bible. And the event we find first is the Passover, the event that took place in ancient Egypt when the Lord God led the children of Israel out of slavery into freedom. When Jesus met for the last supper with his disciples, it was most likely the Passover Feast they were keeping.

But now a new freedom event was about to take place. Jesus told them of a new age to come; he called it "the Kingdom of God." His own death and resurrection would be a prelude to the Kingdom. And those of us who have been baptized and have experienced God's forgiveness have a taste of what it means to be free from the slaveries which still have their hooks in us, to be sure, but which do not have the last word in our lives.

And so, when we come to the Lord's Table, we are celebrating the freedom event of Christ's death and resurrection.

But that is just the starting point. Too often when we participate in the Communion, our thoughts are focused only on the cross, on an event that happened long ago. We neglect the present dimension. But the ritual is intended for our real-life situation in the here and now. It should serve as an occasion for re-affirming both our freedom and our ties to Christ and to each other. The Communion thus celebrates both a past reality and a present reality. The past reality we bring to mind when we hear the words: "Do this in remembrance of me." The present reality we describe when we say: "The bread which we break *is* the communion of the body of Christ; the cup which we bless *is* the communion of the blood of Christ." That is, they are happening now, in the present moment.

We say these words, but because they themselves are rituals, we may give little thought to their meaning. What they point to, in fact, is our ongoing participation in Christ and those who are his. We are not on our own in this faith business. We belong to one another just as we belong to Christ. That is why we kneel at the Table shoulder to shoulder; we are close to each other; we touch. We do not eat or drink one at a time; we do it together. We're in it together. We can't do without each other.

Perhaps we need some new ways of saying this. And so we will make a change in our ritual today. As we rise from kneeling at the Table, we will turn to the person on either side of us, extend a hand of greeting, and say to them: "The peace of Christ be with you," or "May God bless you," or some other phrase we find meaningful. I won't promise we will be doing it this way from now on. But I can promise that we will be giving ongoing attention to the rituals in our corporate life. May God's Spirit lead us.

Mustard Seed Satire

Ezekiel 17:22-23, Mark 4:30-32
Matthew 13:31-32, and Luke 13:18-19

The rather unusual way our New Testament lesson was presented this morning may have given you a clue that something a bit different was in the wind. As you may have guessed, there was a reason for having Jesus' parable about the mustard seed read from three Gospel accounts. By way of explanation, I can tell you that New Testament scholars spend a great deal of their time trying to decipher which of the sayings of Jesus remain in their original form and which were added to or modified by the Gospel writers themselves and later editors. It is a fascinating study, and many times scholars disagree among themselves. Some of the most exciting biblical scholarship these days is being done with the parables of Jesus.

Today we will look at one of them — the parable of the mustard seed. The traditional interpretation of this short parable is that Jesus was illustrating how the Kingdom grows — from the smallest of beginnings to the greatest of results, just as the mustard seed, the tiniest of seeds, grows to become a gigantic tree.

Jesus' listeners were familiar with our Old Testament lesson of the day: a vision by the prophet Ezekiel in which the Lord God says he will make a tiny young sprig a noble cedar of Lebanon, a tree renowned for its stateliness and stature. "In the shade of its branches," Ezekiel declares, "birds of every sort will nest." Naturally, such a prophecy was dear to the hearts of all Jews. Think how glorious it will be, they said to themselves, when God will raise us up above all other nations like the king of trees, the cedar of Lebanon. But notice what Jesus does in his parable. He compares God's coming kingdom not with a gigantic cedar but with a mustard plant, an herb. His parable is, in fact, a satire on the inflated expectations of his hearers. The mustard shrub was a very ordinary plant. There was no way it could grow to tree size, for it was an annual that died after flourishing for a season.

Mark's Gospel tells us Jesus called the mustard plant a shrub, but in their later versions, Luke and Matthew have made it a tree. Mark tells us Jesus said birds would make nests in its shade, but Luke and Matthew have gone one better. In their version, the birds nest in the branches. Why the change? Probably because the early church preferred to "improve" on Jesus' story. They wanted him to describe the coming Kingdom as a grand and glorious thing. So with a few minor adjustments, they turned his biting satire into a comfortable allegory, a reassuring tale to the faithful, promising that God will make of small beginnings a great success.

Who could blame them? We do the same thing. We like to hear stories about little acorns growing into mighty oaks. We like to be reassured that through little acts of kindness, the world will be transformed into a wonderful place. We want to hear that God will bless our efforts here in this parish and make of us a successful church, the envy of all.

Not so, says Jesus. There are no guarantees of success with God. What God promises is that he will never leave or forsake us. That's a far cry from promising success. With the parable of the mustard seed, Jesus tells us that the kingdom is more like an ordinary shrub than a mighty tree offering a permanent, secure home. In the words of Robert Funk:

> The mustard plant does offer a refuge to the birds of heaven, but what a modest refuge it is — in the eyes of the world!
> Man asks for a continent as the paradisaical sanctuary of his final rest and is given a clump of earth.
> The birds, too, have their metaphorical wings clipped: what odd birds they are to flock — in modest numbers — to the shade of a seasonal plant, thinking it to be their eternal home.
> (Robert Funk, *Jesus as Precursor*, Fortress Press, 1975, p. 24.)

We would like it otherwise, of course. We'd like guarantees. We don't mind working if there is a payoff we can count on at the end. We can stand doing the dirty work for a while, but not unless there is a promotion just down the road.

But we find Jesus, to our utter chagrin, setting our expectations on their ear. He is a most disconcerting master, this Christ. As Lord of all, as heaven's king, he invites us to the banquet. We rub our hands in gleeful anticipation. What a feast *this* is going to be!

But then we come to the table. What is this? We are asked to *kneel?* How humiliating! And look at the fare: a measly morsel of bread and a thimbleful of wine. How can we be nourished, how can we survive on that?

Strange host this is! Strange meal. Strange kingdom.

But maybe, by God's grace, we decide to eat and drink anyway.

And then . . . Surprise!

That They May Be One

A MEDITATION FOR WORLD WIDE COMMUNION

John 17:20-23

Usually we call it Communion, and we mean by that word the symbolic meal which we share together, a meal which is the most sacred ritual of the Christian religion. From the earliest times of the church's life, the sacrament of the Lord's Supper has been central in Christian worship. It is variously called "The Eucharist," "The Lord's Supper," and "Holy Communion." Each of these expressions has its own particular emphasis.

"Eucharist" emphasizes the theme of thanksgiving for what God has done for us in Jesus Christ. Certainly a feeling of thankfulness should be in us as we contemplate God's saving activity on our behalf in sending his Son.

"Lord's Supper" emphasizes the theme of the communal meal at which Christ is the host. He it is who invites us to the table with the words: "Take, eat; this is my body which is given for you. Drink this, all of you, this is my blood of the New Covenant, which is poured out for many for the forgiveness of sins."

The expression "Holy Communion" emphasizes the theme of our unity with Christ and fellow-believers everywhere. It is the appropriate term to use on this special day of the church year. For today, around the earth, Christians come together each in their own language, custom, and tradition, to eat and drink the sacred feast. We call it World Wide Communion.

I suppose there are few things more needful in our world than the kind of coming together which World Wide Communion points to. For certainly, there is much that divides the people who live on this planet. It seems to be getting worse instead of better. In the twentieth century, the number of people killed in wars of all kinds has far exceeded the record of previous centuries. Quite apart from war, it is obvious that conflict, intolerance, and suspicion permeate human relationships both across and within national boundaries. Even worse, there are many issues on which people of faith differ, and often these differences cause division and hostility.

What does the event of World Wide Communion say to us as we consider the conflicts separating people? One thing it does *not* say to us is that, when we come to commune, our differences vanish. God loves variety; otherwise, he would have created a world much different from the one we live in. God would have seen to it that people were not so vastly different in their appearance, interests, and temperaments. It is not God's will that the rich variety of our world be melted down so we become all look-alikes, think-alikes, and act-alikes.

What does happen in the Holy Communion, if we can receive God's gift, is that our differences cease to divide us. That which separates us no longer seems so all-important. We see things from a divine perspective rather than from our narrow, provincial viewpoints. And it becomes clear to us that far more important than the things which we have permitted to divide us are the things which unite us.

For, whenever we sit down to eat with another person, we have taken a step toward reconciliation. As we eat and drink together, we are meeting a common basic need — the need for sustenance. When we add to this the sacred dimension, we discover that we share with our brothers and sisters everywhere the common need of spiritual sustenance. Unless we are fed by Christ the living bread, by the Word of God, our spirits die as surely as our bodies die if they get no food.

The Holy Communion is the glory of the Christian church. It is the one place we are united, no matter what our race or language or nationality. These barriers are broken down; we become one in Christ.

This is how we must understand the prayer of our Lord as it is recorded by John the Gospel-writer. Jesus prays that those who believe in him may be *one;* "even as thou, Father, art in me, and I in thee, that they also may be in us." When we stop to reflect on the unity there was and is between God the Father and Christ the Son, we realize what a wonderful unity Jesus was asking for us who are his followers.

It is this very unity offered to us as we surround the table this day. We are joined to each other by a power beyond ourselves — and not only to each other, but to all Christian believers, young and old, rich and poor, black, yellow, brown, and white. But that is not the end of it, nor is it the greatest miracle.

For you see, having experienced oneness and wholeness with Jesus Christ and with each other at his table, we set our faces against everything which keeps people apart, which prevents them from experiencing wholeness. Too often, Christians fail to see this implication. They are content to leave the Lord's table having received the blessing. They forget that no blessing is ever given with the intention that it stop there. And that is why Christians will always strive for reconciliation among all men and women. This striving is the surest proof of the Holy Spirit at work in the world.

Therefore, my friends, as we eat this bread and drink from this cup, may we do so in thankfulness for the unity we find in Christ and in willingness to be God's agents of reconciliation, that we "may be one" in Christ.

The Cup Which We Bless . . .

Deuteronomy 7:9-14a
1 Corinthians 10:16-17

Not long ago during a refresher course at a seminary, I learned that there is something new in the wind in the study of the Old Testament. For the past generation or two, Old Testament scholars have believed that the key to understanding the Scriptures is a theme described by one of those horrendous German terms which theologians are so fond of rolling off their tongues: *heilsgeschichte*. As you might expect, an adequate definition of this term requires at least 375 pages in a book, complete with endless footnotes! In a nutshell, though, it means: "salvation history." That is, Israel's God acted in history to deliver his people out of bondage. The most famous event in Israel's salvation history, of course, was the deliverance from Egypt when Moses led the children of Israel through the sea to safety. We call this deliverance event the Exodus. In the New Testament, deliverance is exemplified by the crucifixion and resurrection of Christ, through which deliverance for all people is made available.

But now a new school of thought has arisen among some prominent biblical scholars. They are saying that there is a theme in the Bible of equal importance to that of deliverance. This is the theme of *blessing*. That is, God not only comes in a powerful way to deliver his people, God also is present with the people, sustaining them, giving them "shalom" — a state of total well-being. The best-known example of this understanding of God is the twenty-third Psalm:

The Lord is my shepherd; I shall not want.

We hear this same theme echoed in our Old Testament text of the day in which the Lord promises his people that he will bless them by giving abundance in the crops they grow, the cattle they raise, and the children they will bear. God will love, bless and multiply Israel.

The word "blessing" has lost much of its power in our time. We use it very casually. Someone sneezes and we say, "God bless you." What does that mean? Hardly anything. Contrast this situation with that of the story of Jacob and Esau in the book of Genesis. When Esau was cheated out of his father's blessing by his brother Jacob, Esau felt that his life was ruined. Blessing in that time carried with it tremendous power.

Scholars tell us that the human practice of greeting — both upon meeting someone and departing from them — has origins closely related to the idea of blessing. For example, the Hebrew word for meeting and leave-taking is the same word: "shalom." This word of blessing wishes for the recipient the peace and well-being that come from God.

As people of faith, we recognize that to experience true blessedness we must rely on our Creator, the God whose power and love called us into being and who surrounds us with ongoing care. One way we acknowledge this truth is closely connected with our eating of daily bread. The proper word for the prayer we say at meal time is "the blessing." We know that Jesus blessed food before he ate. At the last supper he shared with his diciples, he gave thanks for the meal.

The blessing at meal time has two functions, especially at the meal we call Holy Communion. First, it binds those who eat into a community in the sight of God. This is especially important when we come to the Lord's Table and remember that the community of our Lord stretches around the world and even includes those who have gone before us. The second function of the blessing is to offer the praise and thanksgiving of the community to God.

The Apostle Paul, writing to the church in Corinth, uses an interesting phrase as he asks a question about the celebration of the Lord's Supper. Writes Paul:

"The cup of blessing which we bless, is it not a participation in the blood of Christ?"

Other translations render the words: " . . . is it not the communion of the blood of Christ?"

So we see there are two sides to the blessing. The first side is an expression of the continuity between our Lord's first disciples and ourselves. Their last meal with Jesus formed the link between the meals at which Jesus had spoken the blessing during their travels and the celebrations that would make his work present to them again after his departure. He remained with them as the Lord who blesses.

The second side to the words we say when we take the cup is an expression of our thankfulness to God. "The cup which we bless." That is, we offer our gratitude for the gift of ongoing life we have in Christ.

Thus, blessing is mutual — we bless and we are blessed.

And God, in Christ, is at the center.

The Feast of Enemies

Isaiah 25:6-8 and Luke 22:14-27

Ask people to tell you what comes to mind when they hear the phrase: "The Last Supper," and you will probably get as an answer a description of Leonardo da Vinci's famous painting. In the center of that work of art is Jesus, with six disciples seated on either side of him. The facial expressions of the disciples reveal bewilderment, chagrin, or, in the case of Judas, conspiracy; but nowhere in da Vinci's painting is there a hint of warmth or contentment or fellowship.

One biblical scholar has written that this image of the upper room experience is consistent with the celebration of the Lord's Supper in most churches in our own time. For the most part, he says, Holy Communion is "solemn, guilt-ridden, somewhat dull, and blessedly infrequent. The joyous atmosphere of early Christianity, which continued the sometimes raucous celebration of Jesus and his disciples is conspicuously lacking." (Robert Jewett, *Jesus Against the Rapture,* Philadelphia: Westminster Press, 1979, p. 124.)

This idea, that the rite of Communion should include a strong element of joy, may strike you as strange. After all, didn't the last supper in the upper room take place just before the arrest and trial of Jesus? Weren't all the disciples filled with fear as they gathered around the table? And thus, isn't it appropriate for us to be solemn and silent as we remember the sacrifice Jesus made on the cross?

The truth is that the biblical accounts of what the last supper was all about may in fact lead us away from the traditional attitude of Holy Communion as a sober, solemn affair. To get some help on this matter, we must understand something about the old Hebrew concept of the messianic banquet.

The people of Jesus' day lived in hope of the coming messiah, God's anointed one, a son of David. They looked for the advent, the arrival of the one who would ransom captive Israel.

One of the images in the Hebrew scriptures which pointed to Messiah's coming was that of a great banquet. Our text in Isaiah 25 described what would happen on the mountain of the Lord. There would be prepared a sumptuous feast for all people. The wine would be of the finest vintage, and there would be enough food and drink to satisfy everyone. In this prophetic vision from Isaiah, the Lord promises to destroy the "veil" that is spread over the nations. The veil referred to here denotes the barriers to understanding and good will that separate one nation from another, that stand in the way of person relating openly to person and to God. The prophetic vision declares that God will destroy those barriers, and that people who were once enemies will now be able to sit down together in peace and festivity at Messiah's table.

When Jesus came on the scene, he was particularly fond of dinner parties. So much so, in fact, that some observers were scandalized. John the Baptist had been anti-social; John's disciples were well-known for their fasting. But here is Jesus, eating and drinking and enjoying the company of all kinds of people. His enemies accuse him of being a glutton and a wino. But there is more going on in the Gospel stories of Jesus eating and drinking than might first appear.

We get a clue in Matthew's Gospel where Jesus says, "I tell you, many will come from east and west and sit at table with Abraham, Isaac, and Jacob in the kingdom of heaven." (Matthew 8:10) This seems a clear reference to the messianic feast foretold in Isaiah. The enemy peoples from the ends of the earth, who had formerly been barred from eating with Jews, will be welcomed to the table. It will be a feast of enemies.

It is significant that Jesus lived out this image of the messianic feast of enemies in his ministry. He made a conscious departure from John the Baptist, who taught that fasting was a sign of repentance for sin. In John's view, if God could see that the people of Israel were sorry for their sins, why then God might be willing to send the Messiah, who would destroy the enemies of God's people. But Jesus took a much different approach. He sat down to eat with friend and enemy alike. Let's have the messianic meal now, he was saying, and evil will be transformed by the celebration itself.

An excellent example of this strategy is the story of Zaccheus, a tax collector hated by his countrymen. Rather than denouncing him as a corrupt official and a collaborator with Rome, Jesus invited himself to Zaccheus' house for a meal. Observers were appalled that Jesus would do such a thing. They would have preferred that he call for a campaign to murder scum like Zaccheus and all other enemies of Israel.

But Jesus' strategy brought about a voluntary change in Zaccheus that physical force could not have achieved. Feeling unconditionally accepted by this rabbi, Zaccheus dropped his hostilities and defenses. He was converted to caring for his countrymen whom he had been exploiting. He was no longer an outcast, an enemy; Zaccheus was now a part of God's kingdom people.

So we see that Jesus' meals with publicans and sinners were not only unusual social occasions, not only an expression of his sympathy for those who were despised. Even more, Jesus eating with outcasts demonstrated his teaching that sinners are to be welcomed into the community of salvation, and that their presence at the table of the Lord reveals the depth of God's love for all people.

When we remember our Lord's last supper with his disciples, we usually do not give much thought to the presence of Judas at that meal. Jesus knows that Judas will betray him, yet Judas is there, invited to share in the drinking of the cup and the breaking of the bread. Among the twelve disciples were represented many of the divisions and factions of society in Jesus' time. And yet they were brought together at the table.

The Last Supper, which the church remembers and re-enacts again and again, is itself a feast of enemies. It is a foretaste of that time when the kingdom will come in its completeness, a time when all barriers that divide humanity will be torn down, and we will all be guests at God's table, and Jesus himself will serve us.

Do you see what a revolutionary meaning is implicit, therefore, in our celebration of the Holy Communion? It is not a ritual in which only good people are invited to participate. It is not a church rite restricted to members of that church. Nor is the Communion mostly an occasion for remembering the past. Instead it is a meal that points us to the future, to the coming kingdom. Participating in it, we are living by a reality we see in Christ, who gave his life and gives his life for all people — for saint and sinner alike.

To come to the Lord's table, you don't need to be perfect. You don't even need to be good. And that is a relief, because not one of us could come to the feast if the invitation depended on our own merit. It is a feast of enemies; we come to it, and God, in Christ, declares us no longer his enemies, but his friends; no longer enemies of each other, but friends of each other — sisters and brothers in God's family.

There is something else too. In the Lord's Prayer, we pray: "Give us this day our daily bread." The original meaning of that prayer for daily bread was that the kingdom banquet should become a present reality in the lives of Jesus' followers. The literal translation of the Greek is: "Tomorrow's bread, give us today!" It is the bread of the kingdom feast of enemies.

And this means that you and I, as Christian believers, are to pray that the breakfast meal at home, or the snack at the hamburger heaven, or the pot-luck meal at church may all become a celebration of the kingdom. There is to be no division between earthly bread and the bread of life.

For us, every meal, not just the Holy Communion, has deep significance. Every meal with Jesus is a salvation meal, an anticipation of the final feast.